STATE OF IL
Adlai E. Stevenson,

DEPARTMENT OF REGISTRATION AND EDUCATION
Noble J. Puffer, *Director*

How to Collect
and Preserve
INSECTS

H. H. ROSS

Printed by Authority of the State of Illinois

NATURAL HISTORY SURVEY DIVISION
Harlow B. Mills, *Chief*

Circular 39   *Urbana*   *July 1949*
(Third Printing, With Additions)

NATURAL HISTORY SURVEY DIVISION
Urbana, Illinois
SCIENTIFIC AND TECHNICAL STAFF
HARLOW B. MILLS, Ph.D., *Chief*
BESSIE B. HENDERSON, M.S., *Assistant to the Chief*

This paper is a contribution from the Section of Faunistic Surveys and Insect Identification.

(75566—10M—3-49) 2

CONTENTS

Illinois streams are a source
of many insects of interest to
the amateur collector. Shown
here is the Salt Fork River,
south of Oakwood.

How to Collect and Preserve
INSECTS

• • • *H. H. ROSS*

*W*ITH rather simple equipment, the amateur, as well as the trained entomologist, can make a worthwhile collection of insects.

The making of such a collection may have educational and recreational as well as scientific values. Developing this hobby is one of the finest ways for students, especially those in agricultural districts, to become acquainted with the large number of injurious and beneficial insects that they encounter about the home and in the fields. High school classes in biology find excellent laboratory material in the many insects available for rearing and study. Both old and young collectors find a great deal of pleasure in working with the more showy and beautiful insects such as beetles, moths, and butterflies; the satisfaction derived comes both from having welcome relaxation from the day's work and from making real contributions to scientific knowledge. Many entomological museums welcome the opportunity to examine or become informed upon individual, carefully prepared and labeled collections, as these supply distribution records for their localities in addition to other information of value to technical entomologists. Also, the amateur collector profits from his contact with specialists who can identify his specimens for him and advise him at any stage of his work.

It is hoped that this circular will show how easy it is to make a start in insect collecting, and will give the student helpful ideas on how and where to begin.

WHERE TO COLLECT

In late spring, in summer, and in early fall, insects are very abundant in fields and woods, and large numbers of them may be caught by sweeping through the grass and branches with a strong insect net. Flowers of all descriptions are favorite visiting places of many bees, flies, beetles, and other insects, and will afford good collecting. Woods along the banks of streams, open glades in deep woods, and brush along forest edges offer some of the best opportunities for collecting by the sweeping method.

In early spring, when insects can be taken only sparingly in the open, the collector frequently finds sheltered hollows where they may be caught in large numbers. Many kinds of insects live only on a certain plant, and to obtain them the collector must search or sweep the host plant that the insect prefers.

Many obscure places harbor insects seldom found elsewhere. Among these are leaf mold and debris on the surface of the soil, particularly in woods; rotten logs and stumps, which should first be turned over for insects that hide under or around them, and then carefully searched or torn apart for others that live inside; in, under, and around dead animals; under boards and stones.

Trees sometimes yield valuable specimens. If part of a tree, under which has been spread a large white sheet, is struck with a heavy padded stick, many insects in the branches, such as weevils, will fall to the sheet and "play possum." They can be picked off quite easily.

Lights attract large numbers of certain nocturnal insects such as June beetles and many kinds of moths; at night these insects may be collected at street or porch lights, on windows and screens of lighted rooms, or at light traps put up especially to attract them. Swarms of aquatic insects come to street lights of towns along rivers, sometimes in such numbers as to pile up in a crawling mass under each light. Collecting at this source is best on warm cloudy nights; wind or cold keeps most nocturnal insects fairly inactive. Different species of moths and beetles visit the lights in different seasons so that collecting of this type alone yields many kinds of insects.

Insects that live in the water may be collected by the use of heavy dip nets, swept through the water at various levels and through the mud and debris at the bottom. In shallow water, many insects will be found if stones and logs are turned over and leaf tufts pulled apart.

In winter, insect galls or cocoons may be gathered. If these are placed in jars with a cheesecloth cover tied over them, kept in a warm room, but away from radiators and all intense heat, many insects will emerge from them before spring.

WHAT TO USE

For making even a fairly large insect collection only a small amount of equipment is required. A net and killing bottle are essential, and good work may be done with these alone. A greater variety of insects may be collected and with better results if a few more items are added to the list. Here is an outfit that will be found very satisfactory in the field.

1. A strong beating net for general sweeping and an additional light net to be used for moths and butterflies.

2. Killing bottles, several small and one or two large.

3. A pair of flexible forceps, 10 to 12 centimeters (about 4 to 5 inches) long, with slender prongs.

4. One or two camel's-hair brushes for picking up minute insects.

5. A few vials or small bottles containing fluid preservative.

6. Folded papers for butterflies.

7. A few small tins or boxes lined with cellucotton.

These items may be purchased from commercial supply houses such as those listed on page 59. Many items, however, may be made by the collector at nominal cost. Forceps, brushes, bottles, chemicals, wire, and fabric must be purchased, but nets, killing bottles, and accessories may readily be made from easily obtained basic materials.

Nets

Construction.—Nets may easily be made at home. The necessary parts are a handle, a hoop or ring attached to it, and a cloth bag hung from the ring, figs. 1 and 2. The handle should be strong and fairly light. At the net end, fig. 1a, a groove is cut down each side to receive the hoop. These grooves are as deep as the thickness of the wire used in the hoop; one is 3 inches long and the other 2½ inches; and each ends in a hole through the handle at right angles to the length. The ring, fig. 1b, is made of steel wire, preferably three-eighths inch piano wire, which if bent by rough usage springs back into shape and will stand a great deal of hard wear. The wire is shaped, as the figure shows, to form a ring with two straight arms which at the tips are bent at right angles toward each other. The arms and hooks thus formed must be exactly long enough to fit along the grooves and into the holes in the handle. After the wire has been fitted to the handle and the bag or net attached, the joint may either be wrapped tightly with wire, fig. 1c, or bound by a metal cylinder or ferrule slipped up over the arms of the ring, fig. 1d.

The bag, about twice as long as the diameter of the ring, should be tapered at the bottom. It is made from four pieces of cloth, cut in the shape of fig. 2a, and a narrow strip of stout muslin or light canvas, 2b, which binds the bag to the ring. The four pieces are sewed together to form a cone-shaped bag, and around the circular opening is sewed the canvas or muslin band.

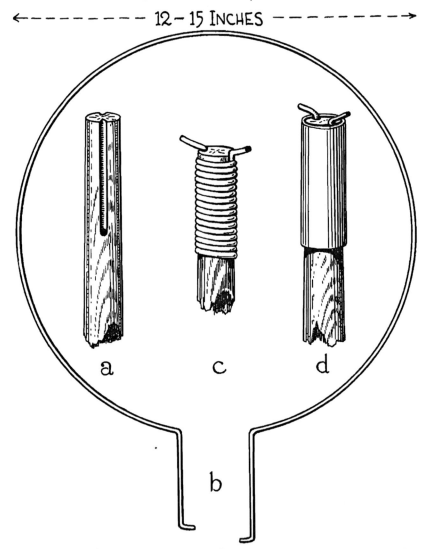

Fig. 1.—Net loop and handle. The short grooves cut opposite each other at the small end of the handle, *a*, end in holes through the handle that receive the hooks of the ring arms, *b*. The ring may be permanently bound to the handle with wire, *c*, or a removable joint may be effected with a metal ferrule that can be slipped up and down, *d*.

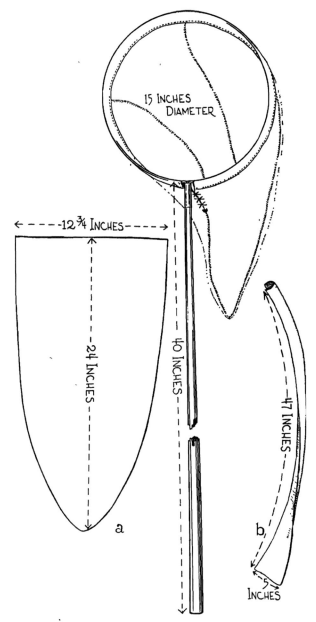

15 INCHES
DIAMETER

←----12¾ INCHES----→

24 INCHES

40 INCHES

47 INCHES

a

b

5 INCHES

Fig 2.—Bag and completed net. The bag is cut from four pieces shaped as in *a*, and the circular opening at the top of the bag is bound with a narrow strip of stout muslin or light canvas, *b*, by means of which the bag is attached to the ring. After the bag is on the ring, the back vent may be closed with a string lacing, as shown in the figure.

The bag may be attached to the handle in two ways. The band may be folded over the ring and sewed down so that the attachment is permanent; or it may be made into a loop and slipped on the ring before the latter is fastened to the handle. In the latter case the bag must be open along one seam just below the handle a sufficient distance to allow the band to slip on and around the ring; this vent may be closed with a string lacing after the loop is on the ring and the whole fastened to the handle. A combination of this arrangement with a ferrule binding the ring to the handle is most convenient, for it allows the bag to be removed at will and a lighter or heavier one substituted according to the needs of the collector.

The first two nets mentioned below will be found to cover all the demands of the average collector.

General Purpose Net.—Ring, heavy wire, 12 inches in diameter; bag, strong unbleached muslin or light duck, 20 to 24 inches long; handle, hardwood stick 24 to 30 inches long.

Butterfly Net.—As above but with a longer handle and a bag of good quality marquisette or fine netting.

Combination Net.—A net that includes the features and uses of the two nets described above and is a better collecting instrument may be conveniently made instead, although at slightly higher cost because of the better materials. Its ring, of 7½ gauge (three-eighths inch) piano wire, is 15 inches in diameter and allows a greater area to be covered with each sweep. The bag, of finest bolter's silk or best quality marquisette, is 24 inches long and serves equally well for the capture of delicate insects and for beating. The handle, of straight-grained hickory or ash, is 40 inches long and permits the collector to cover greater areas in sweeping. If a cheaper net is desired, one of unbleached muslin will be satisfactory for general use.

Care and Use.—All nets are easily ripped and for this reason should be kept away from barbed wire and thorny trees such as locust and red haw. Also, they should be kept dry. Moisture rots the fabric, making it more easily torn. Almost all insects caught in the net while it is wet are unfit for collection.

Flowers, herbs, and boughs should be swept with a sidewise motion. This will collect more insects than an upward or downward sweep and at the same time mutilate the plant less. If care is taken not to damage flowers or foliage, the same patch of plants may be visited several times with profit. The contents of the bag should be removed after every few strokes or sweeps. This practice will prevent damage to the insects that might otherwise be banged around in the net with a large amount of debris.

Killing Bottles

Construction.—The best killing bottles are made with potassium cyanide, sodium cyanide, or calcium cyanide. These compounds give a concentration of deadly fumes sufficient to kill most insects in a very short time, which is desirable. Generally, two sizes of bottles are used, and in either of them one of these cyanides may give good results. Potassium cyanide and calcium cyanide are the most convenient to handle. Only a small supply should be purchased at a time, as they deteriorate rapidly.

A pyrex glass test tube or strong ring-necked vial, about three-quarters inch wide and 4 to 6 inches long, makes a good cyanide bottle of the smaller size, fig. 3. Put about three-quarters inch of granular potassium cyanide or calcium cyanide flakes in the tube or vial. Cover with a tight plug of cellucotton, on top of which put one or two loose plugs. Sodium cyanide is not recommended for small bottles, as it comes in rock form and is difficult to handle. Instead of cellucotton, you may use sawdust and a plaster of Paris batter. In the latter case, cover the cyanide with one-quarter inch of sawdust and over it pour one-quarter inch of newly mixed, thick batter of plaster of Paris and water. Allow the batter to harden for a few hours; then keep the bottle tightly corked.

The larger cyanide bottle, fig. 3, which should be sturdy, may range in capacity from one-half pint to a quart. In the larger bottle, *the cyanide should always have the plaster of Paris covering*. The layer of sawdust and plaster should be a little thicker than that for the smaller bottle. Rock sodium cyanide may be used in the larger bottle if more convenient than calcium cyanide or potassium cyanide.

Label all killing bottles and other containers of cyanide conspicuously with the word **POISON**; keep them tightly corked and away from children or adults who do not realize the extreme deadliness of the compounds. *Never test the strength of a killing bottle by taking the cork out and smelling the contents.* As an added precaution and safeguard to the collector, tape the bottom of the cyanide bottle to protect it against breakage.

The bottle should be almost entirely filled with loosely crumpled, soft paper, which should be changed whenever it gets damp. This paper will help keep the specimens from rubbing against each other inside the bottle and thereby being defaced.

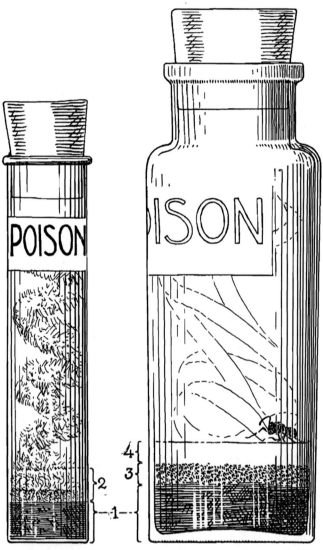

Fig. 3.—Cyanide collecting bottles. Killing bottles of at least two sizes should be included in every collector's equipment. The lethal chemical, 1, is potassium cyanide, sodium cyanide, or calcium cyanide, and is covered with a layer of cellucotton, 2, or sawdust, 3, and plaster of Paris, 4. The rest of the bottle is filled with soft, loosely crumpled paper, which should be changed whenever it gets damp. The bottles should be tightly corked and labeled POISON. The collecter should *not* test their strength by smelling.

Care and Use.—Each collector should have several cyanide bottles and follow carefully these practices.

1. Transfer insects from net to bottle by holding the uncorked bottle in a fold or corner of the net and crowding one or more of the specimens into it, or "running" the open bottle up the side of the net beneath the specimen or specimens. Most insects can be maneuvered into the bottle easily and the opening temporarily closed by the thumb, or the stopper can be put on. In obstinate cases, it may be desirable to stopper the bottle through the cloth of the net until the specimen is stupefied, after which the insect will drop to the bottom of the bottle.

2. Keep small, delicate insects in a bottle by themselves. Such insects as large beetles are apt to mutilate small flies and other delicate insects in the same bottle.

3. Keep a special bottle for moths and butterflies. When these die they shed large quantities of scales which stick to and partially spoil other insects.

4. Keep the inside of the bottle dry. Cyanide bottles "sweat"; that is, moisture both from the insects and the plaster condenses on the inside of the bottle. Moisture will mat the hair and appendages of insects and discolor the bodies. Do not crowd the bottle with large insects, especially juicy ones like grasshoppers. Change the paper frequently. Wipe out the bottle with paper or cloth, which should be disposed of in such a way that it cannot poison persons or pets.

5. Take insects out of the bottles as soon as they are dead. Cyanide fumes soon turn many yellows to red or orange, and also make small specimens brittle so that legs and other parts break off easily.

6. Empty the insects out of the bottles before they have accumulated in a ball at the bottom. To do so will prevent damage to the smaller specimens and discoloration due to "sweating."

7. Discard a cyanide bottle that no longer kills quickly. Substitute a fresh one and you will save untold time in the field. Be sure to dispose of old bottles so that their deadly contents will be out of reach of children and pets.

SPECIAL COLLECTING EQUIPMENT

Frequently, after a certain amount of general collecting, the student wishes to focus his efforts on some particular group such as flies, ants, or spiders, or on a particular habitat. For many such projects, there are special pieces of collecting equipment that are easy to make and extremely valuable in obtaining specimens in greater numbers or in better condition.

Aspirator or Sucker

Small, rapidly moving insects, such as leafhoppers, diminutive beetles, and flies, may be obtained rapidly by using an aspirator or sucker. This is made from either a piece of glass tubing about 1¼ inches in diameter, fig. 4a, or a capsule vial of the same size, fig. 5a.

When made from a piece of glass tubing, the aspirator is constructed in accordance with the following directions.

1. Cut the glass tubing, which has an inside diameter of 1 inch, to length, 8 inches, 4a.

2. Secure two rubber stoppers, 4b, to fit the tubing, and bore a hole one-fourth inch in diameter down the exact center of each stopper.

3. Cut two more pieces of glass tubing, 4c and 4d, from a piece one-fourth inch in diameter. One piece should be 8 inches long and the other 3 inches long.

4. Insert each piece through one of the rubber stoppers so that one end of the long piece projects about 2 inches beyond stopper 4b, the other end about 5 inches beyond; let the ends of the short piece project about an equal distance beyond the other stopper.

5. Over one end of the short tube, tie two thicknesses of cheesecloth, 4e.

6. Over the other end slip one end of a piece of rubber tubing, 4f, 12 to 14 inches long.

7. Into the other end of the rubber tubing slip a piece of narrow glass tubing, 4g, about 1½ inches long.

8. Heat the exposed ends of glass tubing so that the sharp edges melt slightly and round out.

The parts are now ready to be assembled, as in fig. 4, and used. To catch insects, put end piece, 4g, in your mouth, grasp the body tube, 4a, in your dextrous hand, aim the intake tube, 4c, at a bug and almost touching it, and suck. The air current pulls the bug in; the bug usually does not find its way into the intake tube to crawl out. Do not forget the cheesecloth, 4e; it prevents the bugs from being sucked into your mouth.

If a vial is more easily obtained than a wide glass tube, the aspirator shown in fig. 5 can be made. In making this, use only one stopper, 5*b*. Drill two holes in it. Bend the pieces of narrow glass tubing, 5*c* and 5*d*, as shown and insert both in the cork.

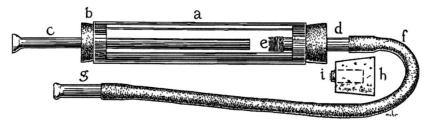

Fig 4.—Aspirator or sucker. This is how the type made from glass tubing looks when assembled; end *g* goes in the mouth, *c* picks up the insects. Shown also is the cyanide cork *i-h*, which is used to kill insects in the aspirator.

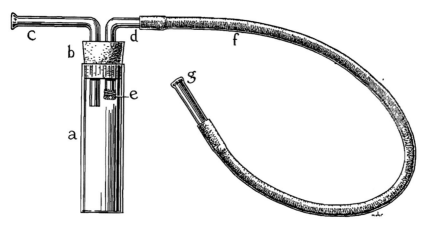

Fig. 5.—Vial type of aspirator. Note the short length of *c* projecting inside the vial, and long tube, *f*. Compare these parts with equivalent parts in fig. 4.

Using a longer piece of rubber tubing, 5*f*, complete minor details as described for the first aspirator, not forgetting the cheese-cloth, 5*e*, and assemble the parts as shown in fig. 5.

To kill insects in either aspirator, use a small cyanide bottle, 4*i*, which is inserted in a cork, 4*h*, that has been partially bored through to receive it. This cork should be the exact size of the tube or bottle for which it is intended.

To use the cyanide cork with the aspirator shown in fig. 4, plug the intake tube, 4*c*, with a tapered paper plug or a leaf, jar the insects away from the stopper at the opposite end, remove this stopper cautiously, and quickly insert in its place the cyanide cork. When the specimens are stupefied, they may be transferred to another bottle. If the type of bottle shown in fig. 5 is used, it is necessary only to exchange corks.

Sifter

Perhaps no special collecting method nets more interesting, rare, and diverse kinds of insects than that involved in sifting rotten logs, leaf mold, and other forest and prairie ground cover.

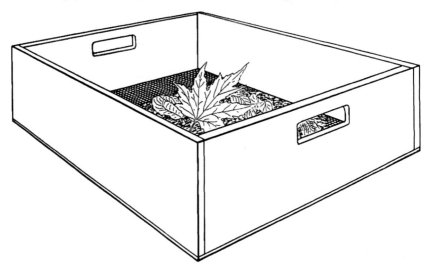

Fig. 6.—Sifter, showing hand grips. Sift debris containing insects over a piece of white oilcloth. Do not fill the sifter more than half full. When you put in a sample, sift it gently at first and then violently. Finally, empty the contents of the sifter on the oilcloth to capture specimens too large to go through the mesh. Patience is required to get the best results with the sifter, which provides one of the best methods for winter collecting.

To do this type of collecting, provide yourself with the following:

1. A stout sifting sieve about 12 by 12 inches and 4 to 6 inches deep, fig. 6. The bottom may be wire screen of any desired mesh; usually 8, 10, or 12 meshes to the inch give good general results.

2. A sturdy piece of white oilcloth about 18 inches or 2 feet square.

3. Collecting equipment, including an aspirator.

Material such as leaf mold is placed in the sieve and this is shaken over the white oilcloth, which has been spread on a level spot on the ground. The small insects fall on the cloth and can be picked up with the aspirator or with a camel's-hair brush.

Many insects feign death when they drop and they are difficult to see until they "revive" and start to move away.

In late fall and winter, sifting is one of the most profitable types of collecting; in any season, it will turn up such things as rare spiders and beetles. It is more successful for large, active insects than for small, slow-moving forms, which are better secured with Berlese funnels.

Berlese Funnel

When you are wandering through woods or fields, do you realize that you are stepping on more insects than you ever see? The ground cover and soil are peopled by a vast assemblage of little animals that are seldom seen by the casual collector. Because many of these animals are exceedingly minute, they are difficult to see and collect by ordinary methods.

The most efficient method for collecting this fauna is by the use of Berlese funnels, named after the Italian entomologist Berlese (pronounced Bur-lazy), who first used them extensively. A Berlese funnel is a very simple apparatus, consisting of a fairly long funnel, suspended wide end up, with a screen placed about a third of the way down the funnel; heat is applied either around the upper portion or over the top of the funnel, and a container of preservative, preferably 80 per cent ethyl alcohol, is placed at the small bottom opening. Leaf mold or other material is placed on the screen, the heat source is turned on, and soon the animals begin to leave the drying sample and migrate downward, dropping into the preservative.

Fig. 7 illustrates a funnel that has proved very satisfactory; it is 15 inches from top to bottom, and the top has a diameter of 12 inches. The bottom opening, exactly seven-eighths inch in diameter, fits into the mouth of a half-pint cream bottle, which makes an ideal container for the preservative. Three angled brackets or hangers are soldered inside the funnel to provide a rest for the screen, which is made of quarter-inch or eighth-inch mesh hardware cloth; the mesh used depends upon the type of sample. A battery of several funnels in a rack, fig. 8, will allow the collector to sample several kinds of material at the same time.

If steam is used as a source of heat, the small copper lines that conduct it act as a partial support for the funnel by encircling it about halfway between the screen and the top; a piece of cloth is tied tightly over the top of the funnel to prevent the upward escape of the animals. If an electric light is used for heating, it should be hung directly over the center of the funnel, no cloth should be tied over the top, and the light should have a reflector nearly as wide as the upper end of the funnel.

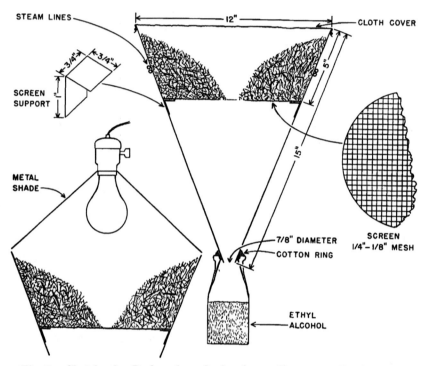

Fig. 7.—Sketch of a Berlese funnel, showing a diagrammatic view across the middle. The central figure shows an arrangement for a steam coil, the lower left for an electric light.

Care must be taken not to heat the sample too rapidly. Otherwise, either moisture will condense in the lower part of the funnel and trap many of the animals working their way toward the bottom, or the heat will kill many of the organisms before they have an opportunity to move out of the sample. An application of heat sufficient to dry the sample in 4 or 5 days is usually satisfactory.

The Berlese funnel is extremely useful for collecting many groups of beetles (particularly Staphylinidae), thrips, Collembola, many groups of parasitic Hymenoptera, ants, mites, pseudoscorpions, millipedes, and centipedes, and a wide range of other minute animals that live in soil, surface cover, logs, or bark.

Collecting Berlese Samples.—Many different habitats and microhabitats provide good samples for the Berlese funnel. You will find that, for general collecting, various types of ground cover are excellent; for leaf mold samples, scrape off and discard the dry surface leaves and scoop up the lower, rotted layers of leaves together with an inch or two of the adjacent soil. You may encounter especially good samples where leaves have blown in along the edge of a log. In such a situation, take some of the log bark with the sample. Collect rotten log samples in large hunks and break them up just before putting them in the funnel. From either standing stumps or fallen logs in which the wood is still too hard to break up, collect the loose bark, as it is often quite productive. Frequently, if you roll a log over, you may find animal runs under it; the debris and earth under and around these runs, together with animal nests, frequently give unusual catches, such as larvae and adults of fleas, and rare ticks. Especially productive are samples taken from the interior of a standing hollow tree; from the bottom of the hollow you can scoop out a foot or more of fine, rotten, woody material rich in rare insects.

Certain specific items placed in the funnel may produce distinctive and unusual catches. Recently deserted birds' nests will give mites and, frequently, rare beetles, flies, and their larvae; mature or overmature mushrooms and bracket fungi are often rich in beetles, thrips, and maggots; bark of living trees may produce unusual thrips, springtails, and psocids; debris from aquatic habitats and from the wet edge of ponds and tiny streams may be productive of rare aquatic and semiaquatic forms. Moss is a good source of peculiar species of springtails, thrips, and beetles; the moss should be rolled up carefully while being transported.

Handling Berlese Collections.—In the field, put samples of leaf mold or other material in tightly woven cloth bags or strong paper bags for transportation. It is convenient to have small paper bags for mushrooms, nests, and other small items, and larger bags for ground cover, moss, and the like. When collecting ground cover and similar material, put in each bag enough of a sample so that it will not shake around loosely, but do not pack it tightly. Be sure that samples do not overheat while being transported.

Samples may be collected at any season. If collected during warm weather, they should be taken to a laboratory and placed in the funnels within a day or two; otherwise, considerable loss of population occurs within the samples. If collected during cold weather, they may be kept in cold storage for a week or two with little loss of fauna.

In putting material in the funnel, lay it carefully on the screen to a depth of a few inches. Moss and sod should be placed upside down in a single layer on the screen. In the case of dense material, pile the sample chiefly around the sides of the funnel and leave an opening in the middle, as shown in fig. 7. After the

Fig. 8.—Berlese funnels in position on rack. In this assembly, each funnel rests inside a double ring of copper tubing (as on funnel at extreme lower left) through which flows live steam. The steam produces the heat that dries out the sample and drives the animals out of it. Cotton or a small rag is tamped between the end of the funnel and the bottle of preservative to prevent escape of specimens.

funnel is loaded, place it in the rack, put the bottle of preservative under it, and apply the heat.

By substituting a different kind of collecting bottle at the bottom of the funnel, you may obtain live material for rearing. The exact changes necessary to obtain live material will depend upon your ingenuity and the type of material you desire.

Equipment for Collecting Aquatic Insects

Night Collecting for Adult Insects.—Collecting at lights on warm, cloudy nights, or warm nights without moonlight, gives best results. Two simple methods are as follows.

Drive your car to a spot overlooking a stream or lake and turn on the bright lights. Into a shallow pan, such as a pie pan, pour enough alcohol to cover the bottom with from one-eighth to one-fourth inch of fluid. Hold the pan directly under a headlight. If aquatic insects are on the wing, they will come to the light and eventually drop in the fluid, which traps them. With a small piece of wet cardboard, you can scrape the entire insect contents of the pan into a small bottle of alcohol, which should then be labeled, date, name of collector, and location being given.

Lights in signs and store windows (especially blue neon signs) near fresh water attract large numbers of aquatic insects. You may capture them easily by dipping your index finger in alcohol, "scooping up" the insect rapidly but gently on the wet surface, and then dipping it in the bottle. An aspirator, or sucker, also can be used with success.

Day Collecting for Adult Insects.—During the day, aquatic insects frequently rest on or under bridges, window ledges, and similar places, and show a preference for the denser trees in shaded situations. They are especially numerous in those spots where the heavily leaved branches hang low over the water and form humid, protected areas in the heat of the day. Here sweeping with a stout and fairly wide-mouthed net is very effective. Aquatic insects may often be picked off stones in such places, especially early in the season.

Collecting for Larvae.—Practically every stream or lake harbors aquatic insect larvae, which may be taken by various methods, some simple and others requiring specialized and complicated apparatus. For general collecting, the following hints may be of value.

  1. Look under logs and stones. Search out crevices in them;

some insects hide away and demand of the collector a keen and careful search.

2.   Tear apart bunches of leaves, roots, and other debris that may have piled up in front of a rock or log, or that may have accumulated at the end of a root or branch dangling in the water.

3.   Pick out bunches of aquatic plants and search through them carefully.

4.   Sift mud, sand, or gravel taken from the bottom of the lake or stream.

5.   Remember that some insects build cases and hide in them when disturbed. It takes a practiced eye to see these without waiting for the bug to dry out enough to make it squirm along with its case in search of its habitat.

SENDING INSECTS FOR IDENTIFICATION

Many insects attack agricultural crops, stored products, domestic fowl and animals, and man himself.   Frequently, it is

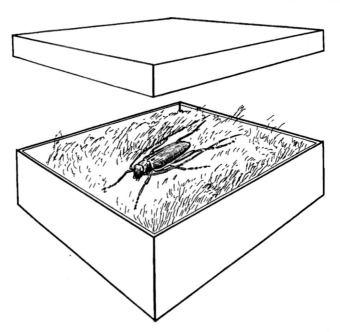

Fig. 9.—Pill box for sending economic insects for identification. Put in enough cotton packing to keep the specimen from rattling about but not so much that it crushes the specimen. *Do not send specimens through the mail in an envelope, unpacked.*

desirable to send these to an entomologist for identification and suggestions for control measures. When sending such specimens, observe these precautions.

1. Do not send insects in an envelope with a letter. Specimens are often crushed or broken beyond recognition if sent through the mail in this fashion and are of no use for identification.

2. Instead, send them in a box, ranging from a sturdy pill box to a shoe box, the size depending on the specimen, fig. 9.

3. Always send full data with specimens, including what they were feeding on when collected, where they were collected, and any other pertinent information.

4. If convenient, send the specimens alive. In this case, be sure to mark the package "live insects."

5. Use a wood or cardboard box for shipping live insects. A glass container will "sweat," and the insects will rot and mold.

6. In sending insects dead, (a) if they are dry, be sure to pack them in the container with enough cotton to keep them snugly in position but not so much as to crush them; (b) if they are in fluid, pack the container to prevent breakage.

7. Do not try to preserve insects in water. Use one of the regular preservatives, such as formaldehyde or grain alcohol (ethyl), preferably grain alcohol.

HOW TO HANDLE UNMOUNTED SPECIMENS

Temporary Cases

If it is not convenient to mount the specimens when they are taken from the killing bottle, the moths and butterflies should be put in "papers" and other insects in cotton.

"Papers" are simply rectangular strips of paper of convenient size folded as in fig. 10. The moth or butterfly, with its wings folded, is placed in a "paper," the edges of which are then crimped over to lock it shut.

For insects other than moths and butterflies, pill boxes or small flat tins containing cellucotton make good temporary housing. A layer of cellucotton is laid in the bottom, a layer of insects placed on it, and another layer of cotton placed over the insects. The lid should fit fairly snugly over all. Cigar boxes and other boxes of like size also may be used in the same way.

Great care must be taken that sufficient cotton is put in the box to take up all moisture in the insect bodies. If the specimens are large they should be allowed to dry moderately before being put in cotton, and placed in a wood or cardboard container that

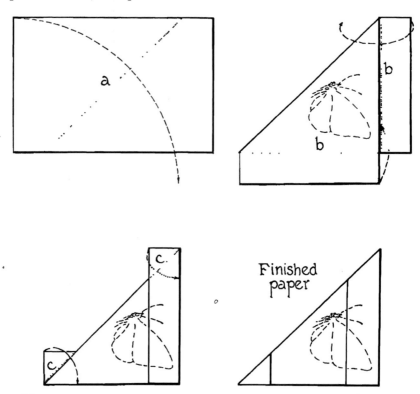

Fig. 10.—Papers. These are temporary means of keeping dragonflies, moths, butterflies, and small insects of all kinds until they can be relaxed and mounted. A rectangular piece of paper, varying in size according to the insect it is to contain, is folded along the dotted lines and in the directions indicated by arrows, as shown in *a*, *b*, and *c*.

will not "sweat," as will a metal box. If the insects become damp in these containers they quickly mold or rot. They should be packed tight enough to prevent their rolling around and breaking.

Relaxing Boxes and Jars

At any desired time the dry specimens may be relaxed and mounted. A relaxing box or jar is easily made. In the bottom of a wide-mouthed tin or jar, put an inch or two of clean sand; saturate the sand with water containing a small amount of phenol (carbolic acid) and place over it a piece of cork, cardboard, or wood cut to fit the jar. The lid must be practically airtight. Place the dry specimens on the cork, cover tightly, and in a day or two they will be soft and pliable enough for pinning or spreading, the next steps toward permanent arrangement of the collection.

The relaxer will "sweat" if kept in too hot a room, and will spoil the specimens. Also, the insects will be spoiled if left in the relaxer too long. The correct length of time varies with each relaxer and can be learned only by experience.

HOW TO MOUNT AND PRESERVE SPECIMENS

Most adult insects in collections are mounted on pins. Such insects as beetles, grasshoppers, butterflies, moths, flies, and bees are pinned directly through the body from top to bottom. Small insects, such as leafhoppers, plant bugs, small beetles, and the like, are glued on card points. Immature insects and the adults of some groups are best preserved in fluid.

Preservation in Fluid

Caterpillars and other immature stages of insects should be preserved in fluid. Grain alcohol at 80 per cent or formaldehyde at 4 per cent are suitable. Caterpillars, grubs, and maggots should first be heated 5 or 10 minutes in water just at the boiling point. This treatment sterilizes the specimens and prevents their discoloration by bacteria in the digestive system.

Many soft-bodied adult insects, including bristletails, springtails, stoneflies, and caddisflies, also should be preserved in fluid. If pinned they shrivel to such an extent that few identifying characters can be seen. The preserving fluid in the vials in which insects have been placed should be changed at the end of the first day or two.

Some hard-shelled insects may be preserved in fluid. Ants and beetles may be thus treated temporarily and later they may be pinned and dried.

Preservation by Pinning

Hard-bodied insects, such as beetles, flies, and wasps, are preserved as dry specimens on pins better than in fluid. The pinned specimens are more convenient to study and they retain their natural coloring better. Flies and butterflies are covered with hairs or scales that clot or break off if the specimens are bottled, and for this reason they should be pinned.

Common household pins are too thick and short for pinning insects. Longer, slender pins, called insect pins, are necessary and may be purchased from various supply houses. They should be of spring steel; a brass pin will corrode and be destroyed by acids in the insect's body. The pins are obtained in numbered sizes, of which 1, 2, 3, and 4 will be found of most general use, and sizes 0 or 00 of advantage in special cases.

Medium to Large Insects.—Medium to large hard-shelled insects, such as moths, beetles, flies, bees, and wasps, should be pinned vertically through the body, fig. 11a. It is essential that the pin pass through a fairly solid part of the body, and to insure this the following standard procedures should be adopted.

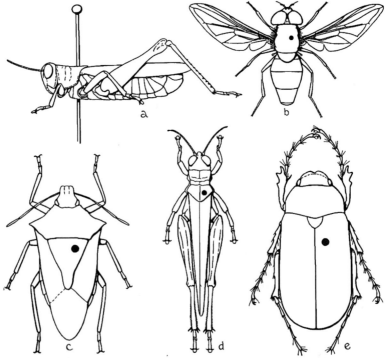

Fig. 11.—Pinning. Medium- to hard-shelled insects are mounted by being pinned through the body in the manner shown at *a*. The black spots show the location of the pin in the case of bees, flies, and wasps, *b*; stink bugs, *c*; grasshoppers, *d*; and beetles, *e*.

1.   Bees, wasps, flies.—Pin through thorax between bases of front wings slightly to right of middle line, as shown in fig. 11*b*.

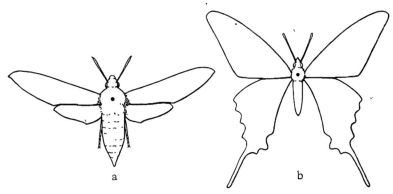

Fig. 12.—Pinning. Moths, *a*, and butterflies, *b*, are pinned through the center of the thorax (instead of to the right of the median line) between the bases of the front wings.

2.   Stink bugs.—Pin just to right of middle line of the scutellum or large triangle between the bases of the front wings, fig. 11*c*.

3.   Grasshoppers.—Pin through back part of prothorax (the saddle behind the head) just to right of middle line, fig. 11*d*.

4.   Beetles.—Pin near front margin of right wing cover near middle line, fig. 11*e*.

· 5.   Moths, butterflies, dragonflies, damselflies.—Pin through the center of the thorax between the bases of the front wings, fig. 12.

The insect should be run about three-quarters of the distance up the pin, but not so close to the top that no room is left for easy handling of the pin with the fingers. It is well to have all insects the same distance from the top of the pin. To insure a uniform distance, the collector should use a pinning block. This

Fig. 13.—**Pinning block.** The block is 1¼ x 1¼ x 2¼ inches, with holes drilled to the depths shown and having diameters only slightly greater than the largest pin that will be used. A specimen is pinned and the pin inserted into one of the holes until it touches bottom; thus the insects of any class, or in any case, may be pinned uniformly at the desired height.

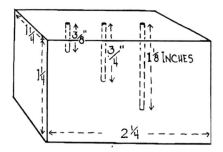

is a small piece of wood or metal usually in the form shown in fig. 13, into the top of which are drilled holes slightly larger than the pin diameters. Such a block may be fashioned of wood with holes made by small nails and covered with a cardboard square

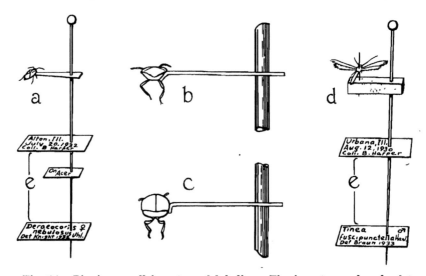

Fig. 14.—Pinning small insects and labeling. The insect may be glued to a card point, *a*, which has been crimped to meet the right side of the body, *b*, *c*; or it may be pinned with a minuten pin, *d*, to a piece of cork or pith, which in turn is regularly pinned. All pinned insects should be labeled, as at *e*. In the case of some small insects, such as tiny moths, the minuten pin may be run down through the body and then into the cork; in the case of others, such as mosquitoes, it is often desirable to run the minuten pin up through the cork first and then impale the specimen on the point of the pin.

through which have been stabbed holes the exact size of those in the wood. The depths of the holes in the block should be three-eighths inch, three-quarters inch and 1⅛ inches, respectively. To use the block, pin the insect and insert the pin into whichever hole allows the specimen to be pushed up the pin and still leave room, allowing for the thickness of the insect's body, for handling at the top.

Tiny Insects.—Very small insects, of which many will be encountered, cannot be pinned through the bodies with regular pins, which will break too many of the insects' parts. Instead they are mounted on card points or on minuten pins.

Card points are small triangles of cardboard or celluloid pinned through one of the sides and crimped over at the opposite apex; a spot of good glue is put on the angled tip, and the right side of the insect is pressed against the glued surface, fig. 14. The slant of the crimp depends on the angle of the insect's side; the desired product is the insect mounted with its top surface horizontal and its head forward; legs, wings, and antennae should be in view and as little of the body as possible hidden by the glue or card point. Very little glue should be used; a small amount holds well and gives a better specimen for study than a large amount. The points may be cut uniformly with a hand punch, and they should be about three-eighths inch long. Good material for making these points is 2-ply Bristol board.

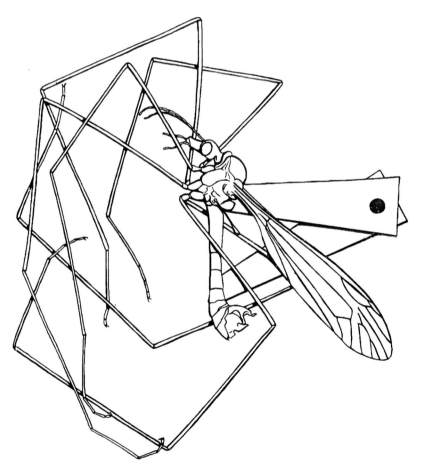

Fig. 15.—Pinning crane flies. Because of their unwieldly legs these insects should have a double card point mount, and the legs should be kept away from the pin.

Minuten pins are short, extremely delicate steel pins, fig. 14*d*. One of these is thrust through the body of the insect and into a small piece of cork, pith, or similar substance, which is in turn pinned in the regular way that a card point is. This method is especially desirable for minute moths.

Insects Hard to Pin.—Wasps, lacewings, damselflies, and like insects have an abdomen that sags readily when the specimen is killed and pinned. This unwanted drooping can be prevented in three simple ways. (1) Stick the pinned insect on a vertical surface of a block so that the body by its own weight dries in normal position. (2) Pin the insect on a horizontal surface and run a stiff paper on the pin beneath the body and supporting it in a natural position until the insect dries. (3) Brace the abdomen by crossing two pins beneath it and thrusting them into the block, allowing the specimen to dry in the angle of the cross.

Crane flies are unwieldy and so are best pinned on a double card point mount, fig. 15. The legs should be directed away from the pin to avoid breakage in handling.

Spreading Board for Moths and Butterflies

Moths and butterflies should have their wings spread before being put into the collection. To do this well it is necessary to have spreading boards that are accurately made but that are not necessarily complicated or expensive.

Construction.—A convenient board for medium-sized insects can be made at home of the following materials:

1.—A hardwood base, 4 x 12 x ¼ inches.
2.—Two hardwood end pieces, 4 x ¾ x ½ inches.
3.—Two softwood top pieces, 1⅞ x 12 x ½ inches, with the top surface planed at an angle, so that the thickness at one edge is ½ inch and at the other ⅜ inch.
4.—Two flat cork pieces, 1 x 11 x 3/16 inches.

Nail the top pieces to the ends so that the slanting surfaces of the tops are uppermost and the narrower edges parallel and one-quarter inch apart, fig. 16. Glue one strip of cork beneath the top pieces, covering the opening between and fitting snugly at each end. Glue the other cork piece flat to the upper side of the base, lengthwise along the middle, and extending to within one-half inch of each end. Finally, nail the base across the bottoms of the end pieces, so that the two corks face each other.

Use.—Before spreading the specimen, relax it as described

under "Relaxing Boxes and Jars." Then pin it, keeping in mind
fig. 12 and the directions given under "Preservation by Pinning."
Thrust the pin, with the insect on it, through the upper cork of

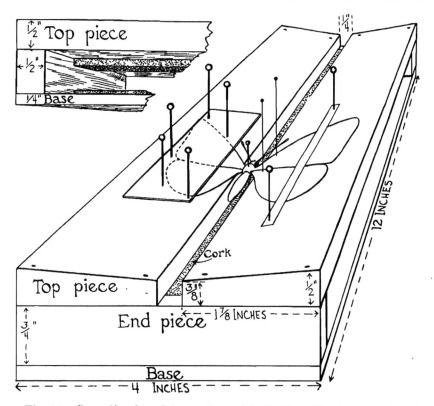

Fig. 16.—Spreading board for moths and butterflies. The insect is pinned
into the groove and its wings drawn forward and pinned temporarily as
shown on the right. The left wings are shown with pinning completed. Inset
is a view of spreading board construction. The top pieces of the board must
be smooth and of soft wood. First grade pine is satisfactory.

the board and into the cork on the base. Insert the insect body
in the groove so that the wing bases are level with the near edge
of the top pieces. Hold the wings at the top level by two narrow
strips of paper and pull them forward until the hind margin of
the front wing is at right angles to the body axis, and the front
margin of the hind wing is just under the front wing, fig. 16. Pin
the wings temporarily in this position by inserting a pin, size
0 or 00, near the front margin at the base of each wing. When
the wings on both sides of the insect are thus adjusted, lay strong

pieces of paper over them and pin them down securely with large pins inserted close to the wings but not through them. Here you may use large common pins, but still better are the large-headed dressmaker's pins about 1¼ inches long. Finally, remove the original adjusting pins and put the specimen in a dry, pestproof container for 2 or 3 weeks. It will then have set sufficiently to be removed from the board.

For good results, spreading boards with grooves of various widths are necessary, and a specimen should be spread on that board the groove of which best fits the insect body. The width of the top pieces should vary to accommodate different wing spreads. The slope of the top pieces should be about as described.

HOW TO LABEL THE SPECIMENS

To be useful to the entomologist and others interested in the scientific relations of insects, as well as to furnish the collector with a complete record of his hours in the field and make more valuable the work he has already accomplished, the specimens should be labeled. The important information to be put on the label is the locality and date of capture, but greater value will be attached to the specimen from a scientific point of view by adding the name of the collector, the host on which the insect was found, or the particular habitat preference.

Labels should be made of a good grade of white paper stiff enough to hold a flat surface when cut up and raised on a pin. Most satisfactory is a "substance 36 ledger." The labels may be printed by hand with a crow-quill pen and black India ink, or they may be purchased completely or partially printed from a biological supply house.

The labels should be as small as possible, and of nearly a uniform size. They should be run about half way up the pin, but not too near the specimen, and they should project from the pin in the same direction as the specimen, as shown in fig. 14.

HOUSING THE COLLECTION PERMANENTLY

Insect Boxes

After the specimens have been pinned and labeled, they should be housed in boxes or cases having a soft bottom or inner layer that will allow easy pinning. Such housing not only insures the safety of the collection but makes for easily handled units once the specimens have been named.

Several satisfactory types of boxes for housing insect specimens may be bought from commercial supply companies. These are usually much better than boxes of home construction, being more nearly dustproof and pestproof. Homemade boxes, however, are quite practical for the beginning collector, due to their ease of construction and extremely low cost. Cigar boxes 2 inches deep or more make ideal insect boxes if a layer of cork or balsa wood or two layers of soft, corrugated cardboard are glued in the bottom. Other wooden or cardboard boxes may be provided with such a bottom pinning surface and used for storing specimens. Boxes of this type, however, afford the specimens no protection against pests, and great care must be exercised in keeping the boxes fumigated.

Manufactured boxes, cabinets, and cases may be selected from catalogs that various firms send free upon application.

Precaution Against Pests

Certain insects such as flour beetles and carpet beetles feed upon dried insects, and unless precautions are taken these may entirely destroy a collection. To guard against them, various chemical repellents in cones or bags may be placed in the boxes containing specimens. Naphthalene, of which ordinary moth balls are composed, is one of the best repellents. A few moth balls may be put in a bag and this pinned securely in one corner of the box, or, more neatly, naphthalene "cones" may be made of the moth balls and pins, and stuck in the corners. To make such a "cone," stick a pin in a cork, heat its head in a flame and then push the head into a moth ball. The pin will melt its way into the naphthalene, which will cool and harden again almost immediately. Neat "cones," fig. 17, can with a little practice be made in this way.

Fig. 17.—Naphthalene "cone." This is easily made with a moth ball and common pin and serves as a repellent to keep away from the collection live insects that might cause damage.

Naphthalene is a repellent only; its odor keeps out pests, but if they are already in the collection the naphthalene will not kill them, and some other substance must be used.

Paradichlorobenzene, called PDB, is a good fumigant to use on pests in the collection. It should be used in a nearly airtight chamber, such as a tight trunk, bin, or case, at the rate of 1 pound of PDB to 25 cubic feet of space. The boxes of specimens, with lids open or removed, should be placed in the container, the fumigant scattered or spread on a piece of cloth or paper above them, and the chamber sealed for about a week.

IDENTIFYING THE SPECIMENS

The complete classification of insects is quite complicated. The entire insect group is first divided into *orders*, such as the Coleoptera, or beetles, the Diptera, or flies, and the Siphonaptera, or fleas. Each of these orders may contain from several dozen to 25,000 different kinds of insects in North America alone. These orders are divided into *families*, which in turn may contain from one to many thousands of species. The family names always end in *idae*, as in Pentatomidae, the name for the stink bugs. These families are divided into *genera* (the plural for *genus*), and the various *species* or kinds are placed in the genera. Thus the house fly bears the name *Musca domestica* Linnaeus; this means that the species name is *domestica*, that this name *domestica* was first applied to the species by a man named Linnaeus and that the species *domestica* is placed in the genus *Musca*. Further, the genus *Musca* belongs to the family Muscidae which, in turn, belongs to the order Diptera.

As an aid to the preliminary identification of his specimens by the beginner and also as an aid in arranging his collection, a short, descriptive synopsis is given below. In this are noted the most distinctive features of the common insects occurring in Illinois. There are rare and obscure forms seldom met by the collector that require a most technical key for their identification, but for these the collector will need to consult some of the more nearly complete books listed on page 58. The collector will find, however, that this synopsis will afford a beginning for his classification of the common forms.

Various characters are used to identify an insect to family, genus, and species. It is always necessary to see the structure of antennae, wings (if present), legs, and mouthparts. Frequently, minute details of these must be examined. Hair or scales covering the body or wings, and the texture of these parts, are important. Hence, specimens should be kept in good condition.

Thysanura
Silverfish

Wingless, flat insects that run rapidly. They have long antennae and three long tails. Terrestrial; commonly found in dwellings. Fig. 18 shows one of the common silverfish, *Thermobia domestica* Packard; its habit of eating book bindings and other starchy materials is well known to most apartment dwellers.

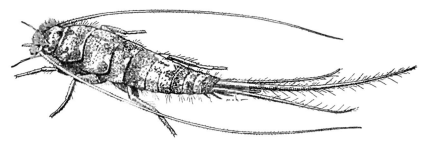

Fig. 18.—Thysanura. *Thermobia domestica*, a common silverfish. Actual length about 0.3 inch.

Some out-of-door forms inhabit wooded dells, where they hide under logs and stones and, when disturbed, run with remarkable speed. Others live in the soil itself and are rarely collected.

Collembola
Springtails

Small wingless insects that jump and crawl when disturbed. They have short antennae and usually a springing foot on the underside near the posterior end of the body. They live in moist places and are abundant under leaf mold and similar material. Illustrated in fig. 19 is *Achorutes armatus* (Nicolet), which often becomes a major pest in mushroom cellars and greenhouses.

About a hundred different species of Collembola occur in Illinois; they include some of our smallest insects. A few never grow longer than 0.007 inch; the largest approach half an inch in length. These hardy animals are active all year and surprisingly resistant to cold. Certain species occur on snow in winter. In Illinois a small bluish-gray species, *Podura aquatica* (Linnaeus), is found on the surface of still water at the margins of ponds and small streams.

Fig. 19.—Collembola. *Achorutes armatus*, a small springtail found in greenhouses and mushroom cellars. Actual length less than 0.1 inch.

Orthoptera
  Cockroaches,
  Grasshoppers,
  Crickets, and
  Their Allies

Insects usually with two pairs of wings, each with a very fine, dense network of veins, the front pair thick and leathery, the hind pair delicate and fanlike. Mouthparts fitted for chewing, with stout mandibles. The young look and act like the adults but do not have wings. Terrestrial insects. This order includes all the cockroaches, praying mantids, walking sticks, grasshoppers, crickets, and katydids. Fig. 20 shows a native wood cockroach, *Parcoblatta pennsylvanica* (De Geer) ; fig. 21 shows the migratory locust or grasshopper, *Melanoplus mexicanus* (Saussure). Several of the groups of Orthoptera have adults that never develop wings. These include such odd forms as

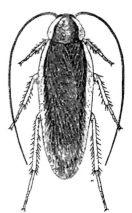

Fig. 20.—Orthoptera. *Parcoblatta pennsylvanica*, one of the common wood cockroaches. Actual length about 0.8 inch.

Fig. 21.—Orthoptera. *Melanoplus mexicanus*, the migratory locust, a common Illinois grasshopper. Actual length about 1.0 inch.

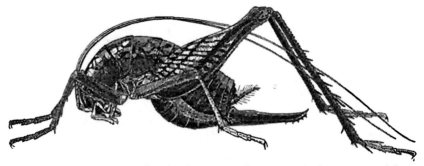

Fig. 22.—Orthoptera. *Ceuthophilus maculatus*, a wingless cave cricket. Crickets of this kind are found in caves, under rocks, and in basements. Actual length about 1.0 inch.

the cave crickets, exemplified by *Ceuthophilus maculatus* (Harris), fig. 22, and the walking stick insects, of which our common form is the tree-feeding *Diapheromera femorata* (Say), fig. 23. In addition to these some species of grasshoppers, crickets, and cockroaches either develop no wings or have only short ones.

Cockroaches are among the most persistent indoor pests we have, and several species of grasshoppers do consistent damage to field crops each year. The sporadic outbreaks of the migratory locust and red-legged grasshopper cause tremendous damage to Illinois crops.

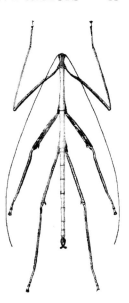

Fig. 23.—Orthoptera. *Diapheromera femorata,* a walking stick insect. Note the lack of wings. Actual length about 3.0 inches.

Isoptera
Termites

Fragile or soft insects with chewing mouthparts. The mating forms are dark brown and have two similar pairs of wings, both pairs delicate and having a fine network of veins. The workers are white and soft bodied, live in colonies in wood, and are called "white ants" as well as termites. They are not true ants. Our

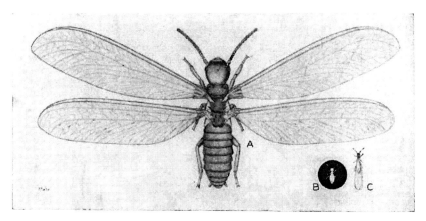

Fig. 24.—Isoptera. *Reticulitermes flavipes,* the commonest kind of termite found in Illinois. *A,* first form queen with wings spread, many times natural size. This is the form that lays the eggs. *B,* worker nymph, natural size. *C,* first form queen, natural size, with wings placed in their natural resting position.

common species is *Reticulitermes flavipes* (Kollar), fig. 24, which is destructive to buildings of wooden construction throughout Illinois; it is most destructive in the southern part of the state.

Plecóptera
Stoneflies

Insects that pass the young or nymphal stage in streams. They have slender, soft bodies, long antennae, long legs, and two long tails, and they move about rapidly. The adults are terrestrial in habit and occur along streams. Most of them have two pairs of wings, which are folded flat over the back; the number of crossveins varies from many to few. The antennae are long, the mouthparts of chewing type but very reduced. Of exceptional interest

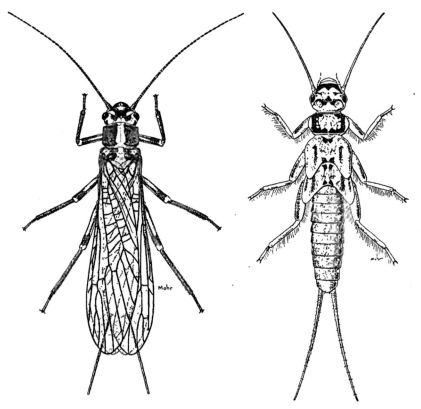

Fig. 25.—Plecoptera. *Isoperla confusa*, one of the typical stoneflies found in Illinois; adult form. Actual length about 0.8 inch. Illinois stoneflies range in length from 0.25 inch to 1.5 inches.

Fig. 26.—Plecoptera. *Isoperla confusa*; the nymph of the species shown in fig. 25. The nymph lives in streams. Actual length about 0.6 inch.

are stonefly adults that emerge in winter and are active on bridges from November through March. Figs. 25 and 26 illustrate *Isoperla confusa* Frison.

Ephemeroptera This order is one in which
'Mayflies the nymphs or young live in streams and lakes; the adults are terrestrial and are found along the edge of the water from which they have emerged. The nymphs are varied in shape and have short antennae, long legs, which are often flattened, and three tails at the end of the body. The adult flies have very long front legs, short antennae, practically no mouthparts,

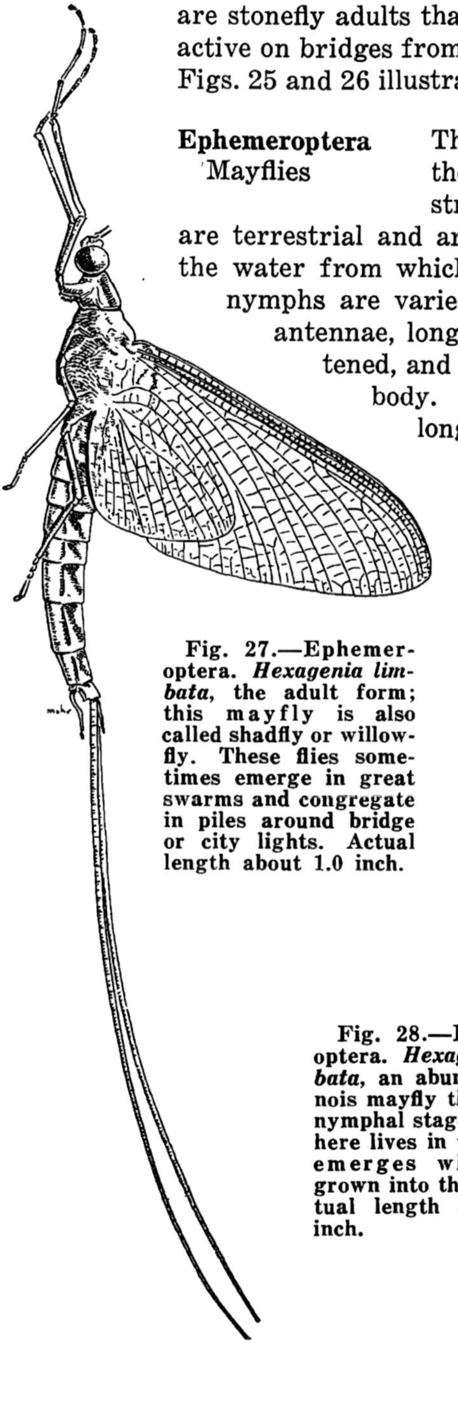

Fig. 27.—Ephemer-optera. *Hexagenia lim-bata*, the adult form; this mayfly is also called shadfly or willow-fly. These flies sometimes emerge in great swarms and congregate in piles around bridge or city lights. Actual length about 1.0 inch.

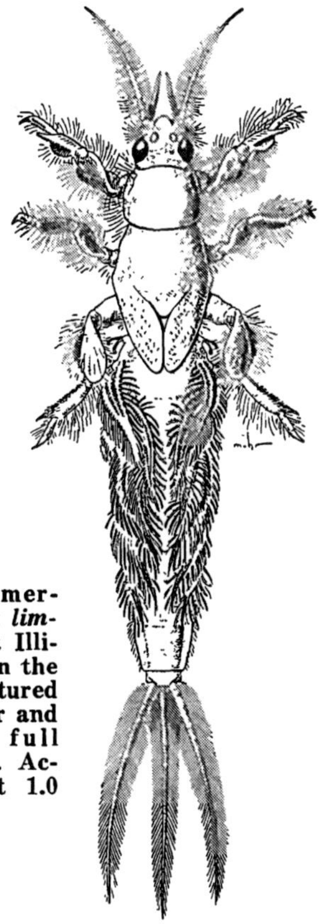

Fig. 28.—Ephemer-optera. *Hexagenia lim-bata*, an abundant Illinois mayfly that in the nymphal stage pictured here lives in water and emerges when full grown into the fly. Actual length about 1.0 inch.

usually two pairs of wings, and two or three long tails. When the insect is at rest, the wings are held together above the body. *Hexagenia limbata* (Guérin), figs. 27 and 28, is one of our very common mayflies and is an important factor in the food economy of many Illinois fish.

Mayflies, formerly called Plectoptera, together with stoneflies, caddisflies, and midges, constitute a very abundant portion of the life of our lakes and streams, and they are important as fish food.

Odonata   In this order, also, the nymphs develop in
  Dragonflies,   streams, lakes, or ponds; the adults are aerial.
  Damselflies   The nymphs have short antennae, long legs,
              and either a stout body with no tail (dragon-
fly nymphs) or a slender body with three leaflike gills projecting from the end of the body (damselfly nymphs). Most distinctive for this order is an extensile "mask," which fits over the face of the nymph and which is hinged to extend forward and seize the small animals upon which the nymph lives. The adults are large, often beautifully colored, as the *Libellula luctuosa* Burmeister, fig. 29. They have chewing mouthparts and two pairs of large

Fig. 29.—Odonata. *Libellula luctuosa*; the adult form of this dragonfly pursuing a fly. Under the water are shown two typical dragonfly nymphs, the lower one with the "mask" outstretched. Actual length of adult about 1.5 inches, wingspread about 3.0 inches.

wings, very finely and intricately netted with veins. The order is divided into two types, the adult flies being told apart as follows:

(a) Anisoptera or Dragonflies.—Body stout, wings broad at base, not folded but held in a horizontal position outstretched from body when at rest. These are strong fliers.

(b) Zygoptera or Damselflies.—Body slender, wings narrowed at base and folded back over the abdomen or up over the back when the insect is at rest.

Hemiptera   Insects usually with two pairs of wings, and
True Bugs   with the mouthparts formed for sucking.
                The order contains two distinct suborders,
the Heteroptera and the Homoptera. In the Heteroptera, containing the stink bugs, chinch bugs, and their allies, the beak is

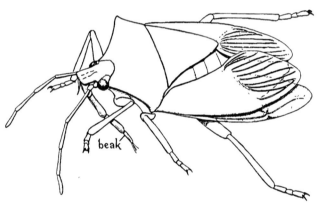

Fig. 30.—Hemiptera. A typical stink bug, belonging to the family Pentatomidae, showing attachment of beak and arrangement of wings. Actual length about 0.4 inch.

attached to the underside of the front part of the head, and the front pair of wings has the base hardened and only the apical portion membranous or delicate; the hind pair is entirely delicate;

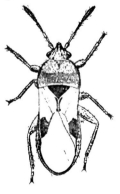

in repose the wings are folded over and flat against the body, the hind pair underneath. These characters are shown in fig. 30, of a stink bug belonging to the family Pentatomidae. The young have the same general appearance and habits as the adults, but lack wings. This order includes many common kinds such as the water bugs, water striders (these seldom develop wings even in

Fig. 31.—Hemiptera. *Blissus leucopterus*, the chinch bug. Actual length about 0.1 inch.

the adult stage), ambush bugs, lace bugs, and stink bugs. Chief pest of this group is the chinch bug, *Blissus leucopterus* (Say), fig. 31. Other pests include many kinds of plant bugs, of which *Lygus oblineatus* (Say) is shown in fig. 32. The bed bugs, another group never developing functional wings, belong here also.

Members of one family, the Reduviidae or assassin bugs, prey on other insects. A few species of these, some of them an inch long, occasionally attack people, inflicting an extremely painful bite and causing considerable bleeding. These are called "kissing bugs."

The suborder Homoptera contains the cicadas, aphids, and their allies. These insects also have sucking mouthparts, but the beak is attached at the back of the head instead of the front of the head

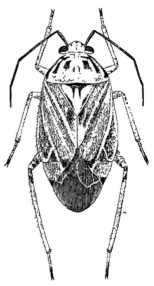

Fig. 32.—**Hemiptera.** *Lygus oblineatus*, the tarnished plant bug. Actual length about 0.2 inch.

as in the suborder Heteroptera. Typically, the Homoptera have two pairs of wings, both of which are membranous. There are probably as many kinds without wings, however, as with them. The nymphal stages are in most respects similar to the adults.

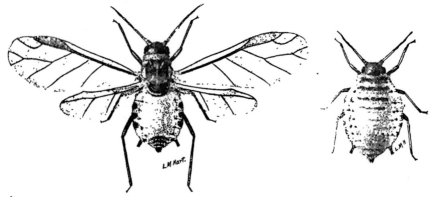

Fig. 33.—Hemiptera. *Aphis maidi-radicis*, the corn root aphid. The form at the left is the winged form, that at the right is the wingless form. All of the plant lice have these two forms. This species, as well as other kinds of plant lice, is frequently attended by ants, which feed on the honeydew produced by the aphids. Actual length less than 0.1 inch.

Sexual characters, and in some forms wings, gradually develop as the insects approach the adult stage, when development is complete.

Fig. 34.—Hemiptera. *Aspidiotus perniciosus*, the destructive San José scale. Note "scale" cut away on upper specimen to show insect proper beneath. Diameter less than 0.1 inch.

Fig. 35.—Hemiptera. *Empoasca fabae*, the potato leafhopper. Actual length about 0.1 inch. This species is pale green. Some species are distinguished by bright red or yellow markings.

This suborder includes a large number of economic pests, such as the aphids, scale insects, and leafhoppers. Many aphids have a pair of tubular structures near the end of the body; these are called cornicles and can be seen in fig. 33, of the corn root aphid, *Aphis maidi-radicis* Forbes. Scale insects usually form a tough scale to cover and protect the delicate body of the insect, as shown in fig. 34 of the destructive San José scale, *Aspidiotus perniciosus* Comstock. Leafhoppers of many kinds,·such as *Empoasca fabae* (Harris), fig. 35, are among the destructive pests of beans, potatoes, grapes, apples, and other plants. The cicadas, tree hoppers, spittle bugs, and lanternflies also belong to this order.

Mallophaga
  Chewing Lice

Wingless, flattened insects with short antennae, short legs, inconspicuous mouthparts, and no tails on the posterior end of body. They are found exclusively on the bodies of birds and animals. The young have the same general shape and habits as the adults and are found with them. Individuals of most of the species move about with considerable rapidity. Many of them are very prettily banded and colored, as is the chicken head louse, *Lipeurus heterographus* Nitzsch, fig. 36. Anyone who has worked with domestic fowls or animals has seen members of this order scurrying along the feathers or hair. These insects feed on what they can chew from the surface of the skin and in some cases are known to injure their hosts.

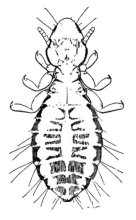

Fig. 36.—Mallophaga. *Lipeurus heterographus*, a chewing louse found on the heads of poultry. Actual length about 0.1 inch.

Anoplura
    Sucking Lice

Somewhat flattened, wingless insects with essentially the same habits as those of the above order except that with their mouthparts, fitted for sucking, they suck blood from their animal hosts. Characteristic of this order are the stout claws at the end of the legs of the horse louse, *Haematopinus asini* Linnaeus, shown in fig. 37.

Fig. 37.—Anoplura. *Haematopinus asini*, the blood-sucking horse louse. Actual length 0.1 inch.

Thysanoptera
    Thrips

Small, active insects, usually about one-eighth inch long, rarely a quarter inch long, very slender, usually with two pairs of very slender wings and with the underneath side of the head forming a sharp, conelike, sucking structure. The wings have a long fringe on the hind margin and the front wings may have one or two veins running the length of the wing. The young of these insects are somewhat similar to the adults but are softer bodied. Fig. 38 shows an adult of *Thrips tabaci* Lindeman, the onion thrips. Thrips suck the juice from plants. They are seldom noticed because of their minute size, but they can be collected in large numbers from blossoms of almost any plant. A few of them, such as the onion thrips and privet thrips, attack agricultural or horticultural plants and inflict considerable damage. A few species of thrips occasionally bite human beings.

Fig. 38.— Thysanoptera. *Thrips tabaci*, onion thrips. Actual length less than 0.1 inch.

Corrodentia
    Booklice,
    Barklice

Small, rounded or flattened insects, rarely a quarter inch long, usually about an eighth inch. Many species have two pairs of wings which have only a few zigzagging veins. They eat fungus growth on bark, dead leaves, moldy grain, damp books, and other materials. Winged forms such as *Psocus striatus* Walker, fig. 39, are found under bark and on dead leaves. Common species found in houses and on stored grain are usually wingless and louselike, similar in general appearance to fig. 36.

Some of the outdoor species become very abundant on drying corn leaves during autumn and may breed in immense numbers. They do little harm, feeding chiefly on fungus strands.

Fig. 39.—Corrodentia. *Psocus striatus,* a common bark louse found on many trees. Actual length 0.2 inch.

Coleoptera
Beetles,
Weevils

These are insects with two pairs of wings, the second pair delicate and folded under the first pair, which are hard and thickened and folded back over the body, touching each other at the edges to form a hard shell, as shown in *Copris minutus* (Drury), fig. 40. The upper wings are not used for locomotive purposes, but form part of the body armor and are

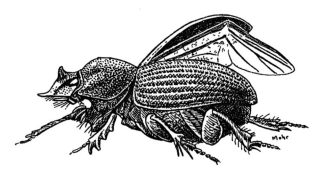

Fig. 40.—Cole-optera. *Copris minutus,* one of the scarab beetles. Note one of the elytra upraised and the method of folding the hind pair of wings under them. Actual length 0.4 inch.

called *elytra*. In most beetles they cover the entire posterior part of the body; in many others they are abbreviated and cover only part of the abdomen. The immature stages of the beetles are wormlike or grublike and have a great variety of food habits. Some of them de-foliate plants, others attack roots, and still others feed on other insects.

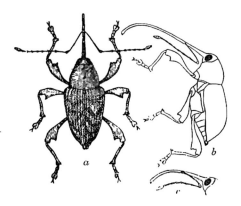

Fig. 41.—Coleoptera. *Curculio caryae,* one of the hickory weevils. Note the beak. In this group it is exceptionally long. In most of the Illinois weevils, the beak is shorter and stouter. Female, *a* and *b*; male head, *c.* Actual length 0.4 inch.

A great many of the serious insect pests, including kinds that attack field crops, stored products, and household goods, are beetles. Beetles of one group that have the front of the head produced into a snoutlike structure, as *Curculio caryae* (Horn), fig. 41, are called weevils or snout beetles. This group has maggotlike larvae and contains many of our worst pests, such as the plum curculio, cotton boll weevil, alfalfa weevil, and clover weevil. Bizarre and striking forms occur in many beetle groups, notably among the scarab and long-horn beetles. The largest in Illinois is the rhinoceros beetle, *Dynastes tityus* (Linnaeus); the male, shown on the cover, has long projections on both head and thorax; the larva lives in rotten wood.

Tree-boring beetle larvae are destructive to many orchard, ornamental, and native trees. These include chiefly the round-headed borers, adults of which are long-horn beetles; flat-headed borers, adults of which are usually flat and metallic; and engraver or shot-hole types, adults of which are small and bullet shaped, and are called bark beetles.

A few families of beetles have both the adults and larvae fitted for aquatic life. Well known among these are the shining whirligig beetles.

Neuroptera
  Lacewings
  and Their
  Allies

Insects with two pairs of wings, both about the same size and shape and intricately netted with veins. Antennae long and slender, mouthparts fitted for chewing, posterior end of the body without tails. The green lacewings of the genus *Chrysopa*, fig. 42, are our commonest members of this order. The young of this order are entirely

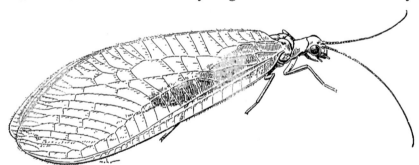

Fig. 42.—Neuroptera. *Chrysopa nigricornis*, a green lacewing. When handled, members of this genus give out a very penetrating and disagreeable odor. Actual length 0.6 inch.

unlike the adults and are grublike in form. They are called larvae. The aphid lion, the interesting larva of *Chrysopa*, fig. 43, is frequently taken in sweeping. Another interesting larva of this order is the doodlebug or ant lion, of Huckleberry Finn fame. The adult insects that mature from these ant lion larvae are very similar in appearance to the chrysopids or lacewings. The larva of each of these insects sinks its long, sharp, curved mandibles into the body of its prey and sucks out the body juices. The female *Chrysopa* has the curious habit of forming a long, slender stalk under each egg; the bottom of the stalk is fastened to the upper side of a leaf. The stalks are thought to have the effect of keeping the first larvae of a hatch from devouring the eggs placed nearby.

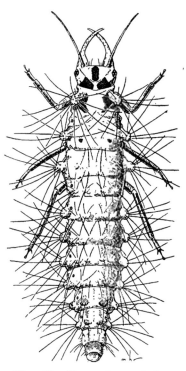

When the larva is mature, it spins a globular, silken cocoon or cell around itself and in this changes into a pupa, or quiescent stage. While the pupa itself does not appear active, within it the larval tissues are reorganized into the structures of the adult, including wings and reproductive organs. When this change is completed, the adult insect emerges from the cocoon.

This order, the Coleoptera, and all the following insect orders differ from the other insect orders in having a pupal stage.

Fig. 43.—Neuroptera. A larva of the genus *Chrysopa*. This form uses the long jaws to impale aphids and suck their body juices.

Megaloptera
  Alderflies
  Dobsonflies

Insects similar in general appearance and characters to the Neuroptera. They have long antennae, two pairs of similar and finely netted wings, chewing mouthparts, and immature stages unlike the adult. All our Illinois representatives of this order have immature stages that live in streams or lakes. Typical of their appearance is the alderfly, *Sialis*, whose adult and larva are shown in figs. 44 and 45. Well known to the fisherman is the hellgrammite, the tough, ferocious, leathery larva found under rocks in streams and prized for bait. This

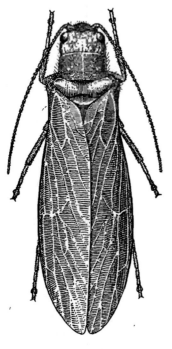

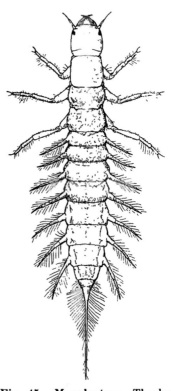

Fig. 44.—Megaloptera. The adult of *Sialis mohri*, an alderfly. Actual length 0.5 inch. Other members of this order reach a length of 1 or 2 inches. They are mostly black, black and white, or mottled gray in color.

Fig. 45.—Megaloptera. The larva of a species of *Sialis*. This form is aquatic.

larva belongs to the order Megaloptera and matures into the large dobsonfly, *Corydalis cornuta* (Linnaeus), which often attains a wingspread of 4 inches.

Mecoptera
Scorpionflies

Insects of this order have two similar pairs of delicate wings, each with a medium network of veins. In repose the wings are laid almost flat over the back. The mouthparts are fitted for chewing and usually are lengthened into a beaklike structure, as in *Panorpa chelata* Carpenter, fig. 46. The larvae, seldom found, breed in damp woods. The adults, usually 0.5 inch long, are active in

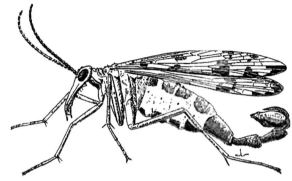

Fig. 46.—Mecoptera. *Panorpa chelata*, one of about 15 Illinois species of scorpionflies. Actual length about 0.5 inch. Note the "scorpion" tail; only the male has this.

early summer in shady woods, flying through the undergrowth. In certain genera the adult male genitalia form a bulblike structure at the end of the body, as in fig. 46; this is harmless but resembles a scorpion's sting, and it is this resemblance that gives these insects the name scorpionflies.

Hymenoptera
Bees,
Wasps,
Ants,
Sawflies

Typically with two pairs of wings, antennae of various lengths, chewing mouthparts; without tails. A typical member of this group is the wasp, *Vespa maculata* Linnaeus, fig. 47. Many adult members of the group lack wings; these include all the true ants, which are without wings except for the sexual forms produced at the time of the nuptial flights. Forms of one species, *Lasius interjectus* Mayr, are shown in fig. 48. The wings, when developed, are without scales, with the venation much less extensive than

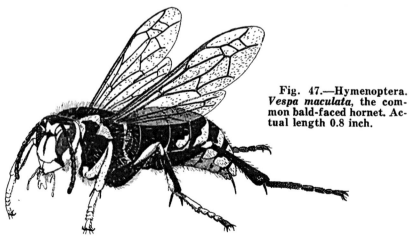

Fig. 47.—Hymenoptera. *Vespa maculata*, the common bald-faced hornet. Actual length 0.8 inch.

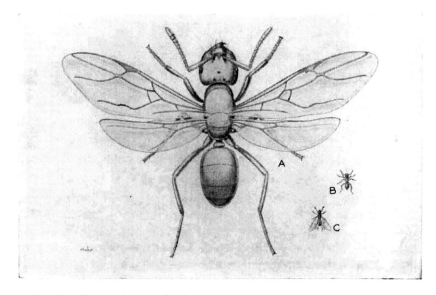

Fig. 48.—Hymenoptera. *Lasius interjectus*, a harmless winged ant, the yellow ant, with which the winged termite is often confused. *A*, queen with wings spread, many times natural size. *B*, worker ant, natural size. *C*, queen, natural size, with wings partially closed and as usually seen. The ant has a narrower waist and shorter wings than the termite. Actual length of queen about 0.3 inch.

in the Neuroptera and with the hind wings different in shape and size from the front wings. The young stages of the Hymenoptera are caterpillar-like or grublike, entirely different from the adults.

This very large order includes such well-known forms as the bees, wasps, and ants. In addition, it includes the sawflies, whose caterpillar-like larvae are extensive defoliators of a large number of native and cultivated plants and shrubs; the large and varied groups of parasitic wasps that exert great influence in the natural control of a tremendous number of other insects; and a large number of gall-making wasps, whose galls are espe-

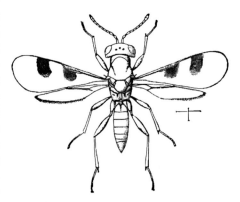

Fig. 49.—Hymenoptera. *Cheiropachys colon*, a parasitic wasp that victimizes one of the bark beetle larvae. Actual length about 0.1 inch.

cially conspicuous on oak trees. A parasitic wasp, *Cheiropachys colon* (Linnaeus), is shown in fig. 49. The parasitic wasps are extremely diverse in size, shape, and habits. They range in size between 0.02 and 2.0 inches.

Trichoptera
    Caddisflies

Insects with two pairs of wings, poorly developed mouthparts of the chewing type, and long antennae; without tails on the posterior end of the body. In repose, the wings are held rooflike over the body and have only a moderate number of longitudinal veins, which are not connected by crossveins into any resemblance of a network. Neither body nor wings are covered with scales. The

Fig. 50.—Trichoptera. *Rhyacophila fenestra*; the adult form of this caddisfly is shown here. Actual length about 0.4 inch.

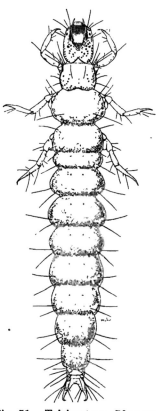

Fig. 51.—Trichoptera. *Rhyacophila fenestra*; the larva, shown here, is aquatic and builds no case. The larvae of some other kinds of caddisflies live in cases made of sticks and stones.

larvae are wormlike and they live in streams, ponds, and lakes. Many of them build cases of sticks, stones, or sand and move about with only the front end of the body protruding from the case. When disturbed, the larvae withdraw completely into the cases and are then very difficult to see. The adult fly and larva of *Rhyacophila fenestra* Ross illustrate this order, figs. 50 and 51. In many aquatic situations, caddisflies are the predominant small animal life and are an important factor in fish food economy. Also, they are stream pollution indicators.

Lepidoptera
  Butterflies,
  Moths

Insects with two pairs of wings, long antennae, and with mouthparts forming a long sucking tube. The body and wings are covered with a dense mass of scales, characteristic of this order, fig. 52. The young are known as caterpillars or grubs. The larval stage in this order is well exemplified by one of the cabbage webworms, *Hellula undalis* Fabricius, fig. 53. Some other larvae are hairy; still others are sluglike.
To this order belong not only a very large number of species, but also a very large number that are especially injurious to

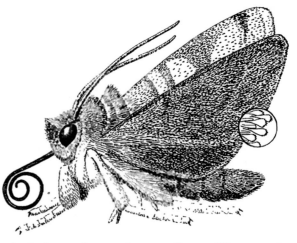

Fig. 52.—Lepidoptera. A typical moth showing scales on wings and body, and the sucking tube, which is coiled up under the head when not in use. Species of this order occurring in Illinois include specimens that vary in size from 0.1 inch to several inches. The largest of these insects have a wingspread of over 5 inches.

agriculture. These include such species as the codling moth, cabbage moth, butterflies, the entire cutworm group, and a host of others. In addition, the various clothes moths, which are a constant source of loss to householders, and various species of meal moths, which cause tremendous damage to stored grain every year, are members of this order.

In one group of moths, there are clear "windows" on the wings, but these are always surrounded by areas or lines of scales. A few species of the Lepidoptera are very odd in having wingless

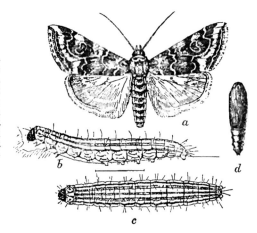

Fig. 53.—Lepidoptera. *Hellula undalis*, one of the cabbage webworms; *a,* adult; *b,* larva, side view; *c,* larva, top view; *d,* the pupa or transformation stage from which the adult emerges. The actual length of the adult insect is about 0.3 inch; its wingspread is about 0.8 inch.

females. Examples are the bagworms and some of the cankerworms. In these species, however, the body of the female is densely clothed with scales, which will serve to identify her as one of the Lepidoptera.

The habits of Lepidoptera larvae are very diverse. Most of these larvae are leaf eaters, but some bore into trunks of trees and stems of plants. Some of the small ones mine within leaf tissue, others live in the ground, where they eat roots, and a few are aquatic, living in clear, rapidly flowing streams.

Diptera
Flies,
Mosquitoes,
and Their
Allies

Insects with only *one pair of wings,* these with only a limited number of veins. Other characters of the order, including antennae and mouthparts, are extremely varied. Most immature stages are wormlike or maggotlike and always live in some protected situation such as within the tissues of a plant, in water, in leaf mold, or in the tissues of animals. A typical life cycle is that shown for the common onion maggot, *Hylemyia antiqua* (Meigan), fig. 54. The ubiquitous house fly is undoubtedly the best known representative of this order. It is also one of our most persistent and dangerous insect pests, when its record as a possible carrier of many diseases and internal parasites is considered.

Mosquitoes, punkies, black flies, and horse flies are equally well-known members of this order. Mosquitoes are probably the most annoying single group of insects. In addition to economic forms, the order Diptera includes midges, crane flies, bee flies,

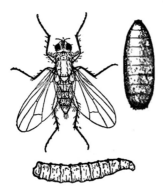

Fig. 54.—Diptera. *Hylemyia antiqua*, the onion maggot. Note the fly with only a single pair of wings, the maggotlike larva without legs, and the darker, egg-shaped pupa or quiescent stage. The larvae feed on the roots, bulbs, and stems of the onion plants, and the pupae are formed in the soil around the roots. The· adult flies emerge and lay eggs at the base of the plants or in nearby cracks in the soil.

robber flies, bluebottle flies, and a great assortment of other different kinds of insects.

Interesting are the bee flies, which mimic other ·insects such as honey bees, bumble bees, and wasps to an extent that wins them immunity from the attention of many beginning collectors.

Siphonaptera
Fleas
Wingless insects that are conspicuously flattened sideways; with stout, spiny legs, and with numerous spines over the body; without conspicuous antennae or tails or a forked posterior appendage like that of the springtails; usually hard; ranging in color from yellowish brown to almost black. The cat and dog flea, *Ctenocephalides canis* (Curtis), is shown in fig. 55. All the fleas, which

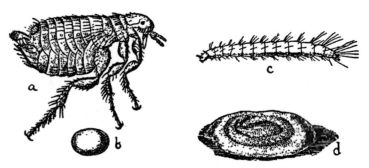

Fig. 55.—Siphonaptera. *Ctenocephalides canis*, cat and dog flea: *a*, the adult; *b*, the egg; *c*, the wormlike larva; and, *d*, the pupa. Actual length of adult about 0.1 inch.

feed on the blood of birds and other animals, have sucking mouth-parts. They are powerful jumpers. The young stages are slender, white worms, which live in the nests of various animals; these larvae are seldom collected. The fleas are found on the animals themselves or around their nests. Several species of fleas, includ-ing the cat and dog flea, the human flea, and the rat fleas, attack man. One of the rat fleas, *Xenopsylla cheopis* (Rothschild), is of especial importance because it is the common transmitter of bubonic plague.

RELATIVES OF INSECTS

There are many small animals that belong to the same general group as insects and that are frequently collected with them. Spiders, centipedes, and amphipods are a few of many examples of such animals. Together with insects they form the animal phylum called Arthropoda, characterized by having seg-mented bodies and jointed legs. A brief description is included here of the commoner groups of these insect relatives found in Illinois.

Isopoda
  Sow Bugs,
  Pill Bugs

These animals are convex, many legged, and have conspicuous antennae; several of the posterior segments are short and joined rather closely to form an abdomen. Of the Illinois forms, about one-half are aquatic, living in streams and ponds. The others live in terrestrial situa-tions that are humid and dark. They are frequently found under boards and in soil in greenhouses. One species of this group is *Porcellionides pruinosus* (Brandt), fig. 56. Many of the terrestrial forms possess the ability to curl up in a hard shell-like ball when disturbed. These animals, rela-tives of crabs, shrimps and crayfish, belong to the general group known as crustaceans. The crustacean groups are abundant in the ocean. In past geologic ages, the early ancestors of such predominantly terres-trial groups as insects and spiders re-sembled ancestors of the present crusta-cean marine forms.

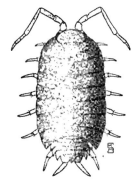

Fig. 56.—Isopoda. *Porcellionides pruino-sus*, a common green-house sow bug. Actual length 0.3 inch.

Amphipoda
Small Water
Shrimps

These humpbacked, many-legged animals, fig. 57, are also crustaceans, but unlike the isopods they are flattened sideways like a flea. They are all aquatic but are seldom found swimming in open water; they prefer to live in tangled masses of vegetation, under stones or logs, and among debris in the very shallow water where it touches the bank. These little shrimps are never more than about one-half an inch long and are frequently collected in large numbers along with aquatic beetles.

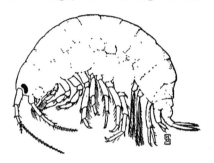

Fig. 57.—Amphipoda. *Gammarus* sp., a common small water shrimp. Actual length 0.4 inch.

Pseudoscorpionida
Pseudoscorpions

The pseudoscorpions, which belong to the spider group, are characterized by a pair of stout pinchers at the end of the front legs, as in *Larca granulata* (Banks), fig. 58. They have short, stout bodies, each with five pairs of legs including the chelate front pair, but unlike the true scorpions they have no tails or stings. The pseudoscorpions are sometimes found indoors in old books, looking for their prey of small insects. They occur in greater numbers in wooded areas.

Fig. 58.—Pseudoscorpionida, *Larca granulata*, a native Illinois pseudoscorpion. Actual length 0.1 inch.

Phalangida
Daddy Longlegs,
Harvestmen

Spider-like forms, each animal with a short, round body and four pairs of walking legs that in most species are very long, fig. 59. They occur chiefly in woods and may be found in numbers walking over foliage, logs, and bluffs. They

Fig. 59.—Phalangida. A common harvestman or daddy longlegs. Actual length of body 0.3 inch.

feed on decaying humus. A few Illinois forms occur chiefly on bark and these have considerably shorter legs than the species that range more widely.

Araneida
  Spiders

These varied and well-known animals have four pairs of walking legs and a body divided into a cephalothorax (which combines the head and thorax) and abdomen. The spiders present a tremendous variety of shapes, some being round and fat, as in the case of the black widow, *Latrodectus mactans* Fabricius, fig. 60, others being long and slender, mimicking ants. Others are crab-like in shape; some that are long and slender are extremely rapid in their movements. Spiders appear practically everywhere. Certain species are definitely domestic and are found only in houses. In Illinois the only poisonous species of any importance is the black widow spider, which is found in a variety of situations.

Fig. 60.—Araneida. *Latrodectus mactans*, the black widow spider. Actual length of body 0.4 inch.

Acarina
  Ticks,
  Mites

Unlike the spiders, members of this group have usually no marked division between the cephalothorax and the abdomen. Each adult has four pairs of walking legs, although an individual of the very young stages has only three pairs. The mites are generally very minute and seldom are seen by the beginning collector. They vary greatly in general appearance. Many species are extremely destructive to stored products, to live domestic animals, and to many groups of plants. Adults of the harvest mite

Fig. 61.—Acarina. *Dermacentor variabilis*, the common dog tick of Illinois and vector of Rocky Mountain spotted fever. When engorged, the tick looks like a red berry. Actual length 0.2 inch. (After Bishopp.)

and early stages of the chigger mite attack man persistently. Ticks are larger than mites and all the species feed on warm-blooded animals, including birds and mammals. Our commonest Illinois species is *Dermacentor variabilis* (Say), fig. 61, which transmits the often fatal disease called Rocky Mountain spotted fever. Although this disease occurs only infrequently in Illinois, hikers and others exposed to ticks should be very careful to remove ticks from their clothing and bodies after every excursion into the out-of-doors.

Diplopoda
Millipedes

This group comprises the "thousand legged worms," which are not worms at all but members of the same general group as cray-fish and insects. The millipedes have a distinct head and a long body with two pairs of legs on every segment. Our commonest representative is the large *Parajulus impressus* (Say), fig. 62, a robust, cylindrical, reddish species commonly found in rotten logs or moist leaf mold. Most species feed on decaying vegetable matter. A few occasionally do considerable damage in greenhouses.

Fig. 62.—Diplopoda. *Parajulus impressus*, common Illinois millipede. Actual length 1.5 inches.

Chilopoda
Centipedes

Elongate animals, similar in general appearance to the millipedes but with only one leg on each body segment. Many species are predaceous, feeding on insects and other small animals in rotten logs and humus. Most familiar to the city dweller is the house centipede, *Scutigera forceps* Rafinesque, fig. 63; this is a common inhabitant of dark places in houses, where it runs about with incredible speed in its search for small insects upon which it feeds. Other species may be encountered under boards and stones in gardens. Some Illinois centipedes found in woody or rocky situations

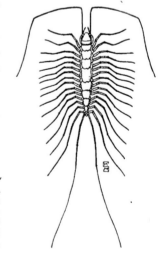

Fig. 63.—Chilopoda. *Scutigera forceps*, the house centipede, commonly found in dark basements. Actual length of body 1.0 inch.

are 2 inches or more long. No chilopod group in this state is dangerous to human beings, but to the south occur centipedes nearly a foot long that may inflict serious bites.

THE STATE INSECT COLLECTION

Illinois is one of the very few states that maintains a large research insect collection. This collection is under the care and guidance of the Section of Faunistic Surveys and Insect Identi-

Fig. 64.—The Natural Resources Building, home of the Illinois Natural History Survey, houses the state insect collection. This picture does not show the new building wings, begun in December, 1947.

fication of the Illinois Natural History Survey. It is housed in the west part of the fireproof Natural Resources Building on the University of Illinois campus at Urbana, fig. 64. Begun about 1880, the collection has grown steadily until now it is the most extensive representative collection of the insect fauna of any single state in the nation. The collection consists of over 2,000,000 specimens of insects housed in steel cabinets, fig. 65. The pinned collection includes about 500,000 specimens in trays. The alcoholic collection contains over 1,500,000 insects, including not only a great amount of valuable adult material but also a very useful collection of immature insects. The slide collection contains nearly 70,000 specimens mounted as permanent microscopic perparations.

The most important use of the collection is in the identification of insects known to damage crops, stored grains, and household articles, or to threaten human health. Important also is its use as a storehouse of information regarding the ecology, host relationships, and distribution of Illinois insects.

For maximum usefulness, the collection should contain a complete representation of the Illinois insect fauna, supplement-

Fig. 65.—A view in the collection room of the Illinois Natural History Survey. In the steel cabinets and hardwood trays shown here are arranged the pinned insect specimens. Similar cabinets contain material in liquid preservative. Adjoining the collection room are the offices and laboratories of the Section of Faunistic Surveys and Insect Identification, where records of insect distribution and habits are kept on file.

ed with as much additional North American material as can be obtained. This additional comparison material is frequently necessary to evaluate correctly the species occurring in the state. It is estimated that there are about 18,000 different species of insects in Illinois and 80,000 in North America. The collection contains representatives of over 13,000 Illinois species, and a great many other North American species useful as comparison material in the identification of Illinois forms.

So large is the field of insect classification that many important gaps exist in our knowledge of the Illinois fauna. Gifts to the collection of well-prepared material are greatly appreciated.

Many of those already received have filled important gaps in the collection and added valuable records to the Survey files of insect distribution.

HOW TO SHIP A COLLECTION

Specimens which the collector is unable to name should be sent to specialists or entomological museums for determination. The arrangements under which these specialists will undertake the work vary, but experts often will study well preserved and labeled collections in return for duplicate specimens which they may keep. However, the identification of many insects is so difficult and laborious that rapid service is not always to be expected by collectors sending in material.

The collection needs special preparation and care to guard against breakage if it is to be shipped to an authority for determination.

See that all pins are thrust securely into the cork on the bottom of the box. Thrust extra pins of the same height in each corner and over the whole lay a piece of thin cardboard that has been cut to fit the inside of the box snugly; then place over this a layer of cotton wool or cellucotton thick enough to press firmly against the cardboard when the top is closed. Wrap the box in paper and then pack it in a larger box, protected on all sides by a layer of excelsior or crumpled paper at least 2 inches thick.

REPORTS ON ILLINOIS INSECTS

As a result of the accumulation of material and information in the faunistic collection, the Illinois Natural History Survey is publishing a series of reports dealing with various groups of insects and other animals in Illinois. These reports are designed primarily for use of the advanced student in zoology and entomology. They contain information regarding the characteristics, habits, and distribution of the various species in the state, keys for their identification, and illustrations to assist in diagnosis of the characters used. Because of their great relative abundance in regard to both species and numbers, and their importance as pests, insects have received a great deal of attention and much has been written about them. In most cases good microscopic equipment is necessary to see clearly the characters used in the species diagnosis of insects. The following reports of Illinois insects are available at the present time. These reports are published in the Bulletin series of the Natural History Survey and can be obtained by sending an order together with the proper remittance to the Illinois Natural History Survey, Urbana, Illinois.

The Plant Lice, or Aphiidae, of Illinois, by Frederick C. Hottes and Theodore H. Frison. $1.25.

The Dermaptera and Orthoptera of Illinois, by Morgan Hebard. $1.00.

The Stoneflies, or Plecoptera, of Illinois, by Theodore H. Frison. $1.25.

Studies of North American Plecoptera, With Special Reference to the Fauna of Illinois, by Theodore H. Frison. $1.00.

The Plant Bugs, or Miridae, of Illinois, by Harry H. Knight. $1.25.

The Caddis Flies, or Trichoptera, of Illinois, by Herbert H. Ross. $1.50.

The Mosquitoes of Illinois (Diptera, Culicidae), by Herbert H. Ross. 50 cents.

The Leafhoppers, or Cicadellidae, of Illinois, by D. M. DeLong. $1.25.

The Pseudoscorpions of Illinois, by C. Clayton Hoff. 50 cents.

USEFUL BOOKS

There is a considerable number of books that can be of great help to the beginner in naming his specimens. The following are perhaps the most easily used. Others are being published from time to time.

An Introduction to Entomology, by J. H. Comstock. The Comstock Publishing Company, Ithaca, N. Y.

The Butterfly Book, by W. J. Holland. Doubleday, Doran & Company, Garden City, N. Y.

The Moth Book, by W. J. Holland. Doubleday, Page & Company, Garden City, N. Y. Out of print but may be obtained from secondhand book dealers.

Field Book of Insects, by Frank E. Lutz. G. P. Putnam's Sons, New York, N. Y.

Destructive and Useful Insects, by C. L. Metcalf and W. P. Flint. McGraw-Hill Book Company, 370 Seventh Avenue, New York, N. Y.

Field Book of Ponds and Streams, by Ann Haven Morgan. G. P. Putnam's Sons, New York, N. Y.

The Insect Guide, by Ralph B. Swain. Doubleday & Company, Inc., Garden City, N. Y.

College Entomology, by E. O. Essig. The Macmillan Company, New York, N. Y.

Entomology for Introductory Courses, by Robert Matheson. The Comstock Publishing Company, Ithaca, N. Y.

A Textbook of Entomology, by Herbert H. Ross. John Wiley & Sons, Inc., 440 Fourth Ave., New York, N. Y.

WHERE TO BUY SUPPLIES

The following list, by no means complete, contains names and addresses of companies that furnish entomological supplies. Most of these companies will send catalogs and price lists on request.

American Optical Company, Scientific Instrument Division. Buffalo 15, N. Y.

Bausch and Lomb Optical Company. 626 St. Paul Street, Rochester 2, N. Y.

Central Scientific Company. 1700 Irving Park Boulevard, Chicago 13, Ill.

General Biological Supply House, Inc. 761-763 East Sixty-ninth Place, Chicago 37, Ill.

E. H. Sargent and Company. 155-65 East Superior Street, Chicago 11, Ill.

Ward's Natural Science Establishment, Inc. P. O. Box 24, Beechwood Station, Rochester 9, N. Y.

CPSIA information can be obtained at www.ICGtesting.com
Printed in the USA
LVOW07s1039231015

459482LV00033B/1886/P